Planet Earth

Polar Regions

Steve Parker

QED Publishing

Copyright © QED Publishing 2008

First published in the UK in 2008 by
QED Publishing
A Quarto Group company
The Old Brewery, 6 Blundell Street,
London, N7 9BH

www.qed-publishing.co.uk

A catalogue record for this book is available from
the British Library.

ISBN 978 1 84835 060 1

Author Steve Parker
Design and Editorial East River Partnership

Publisher Steve Evans
Creative Director Zeta Davies

Printed and bound in China

Picture credits
(t = top, b = bottom, l = left, r = right,
c = centre, FC = front cover)

Corbis 19t Bettmann, 24–25, 25b Tim Davis, 25t
Rick Price, 28–29 Reuters, 29r Karen Kasmauski
Getty Images 1, 16 Tom Vezo, 6t Jeff Harbers, 11t
Jorn Georg Tomter, 12–13t Daniel J Cox, 14t Brian
J Skerry, 15t, 16–17, 21 Flip Nicklin, 20–21 Tui De
Roy, 21t Bill Curtsinger, 27 Stuart Westmorland
NHPA 5, 23b, 27t Bryan & Cherry Alexander
Photolibrary 14–15 Doug Perrine, 18 David B
Fleetham, 20t Roland Birke, 21t James Watt,
22–23 Kevin Schafer, 26–27 Doug Allen
Photoshot 10–11 Fergus Gill
Shutterstock 1, 2–3, 30–31, 32 Chris Howey/
1 Eric Isselée, 1 Vladimirs Koskins, 1, 31 Charlie
Bishop, 1, 8t James R Hearn, 3, 16t Halldor
Eiriksson, 4b Stasys Eidiejus, 4–5, 22t Jan Martin
Will, 6–7, 19b, 22–23 Armin Rose, 8b Andreas
Gradin, 8–9 TTphoto, 9t Roman Krochuk,
10t Naturablichter, 11b, 13t, 13b Gail Johnson,
12–13b Sam Chadwick, 14–15 Edward Chin,
18–19 Vera Bogaerts, 28–29t Steve Estvanik,
30 Sandy Buckley

Words in bold are
explained in the
glossary on page 30.

Contents

Top and bottom

At the top of the world is the North Pole, and at the bottom is the South Pole. These places are cold in summer and very, very cold in winter.

Summer and winter

On Earth, the furthest points in the north and south are called the poles. The Arctic is in the far north, around the North Pole, and the Antarctic is in the far south, around the South Pole. These areas are very cold and are mainly covered in ice. Even though the sun never sets in summer, it remains cold because the sun's rays are low in the sky and weak. In winter, the sun never rises and it is freezing cold.

Polar bears live in the Arctic region around the North Pole.

The Earth's poles lie at opposite ends of the world and appear icy white when seen from space.

North Pole

South Pole

Wow!

At the North Pole, the sun rises around 21 March and does not set again for six months. At the South Pole, the sun does not rise for six months from 21 March.

Traditionally, Inuit people of the far north catch fish through ice holes.

It's so... c-c-cold!

The coldest temperature recorded, minus 89°C, was in the Antarctic. That is four times colder than a household freezer!

Life in the cold

Even in these harsh places, there is life. Fish, seals, penguins and whales swim in the seas. Small plants, such as mosses and herbs, grow in the Arctic. People live here, too.

Arctic Ocean

EUROPE

ASIA

NORTH AMERICA

AFRICA

SOUTH AMERICA

OCEANIA

Antarctic

The Arctic: frozen ocean

There is no land at the North Pole, not even within many hundreds of kilometres around the Pole. Much of the Arctic is a cold, shallow ocean. This is covered with ice during the long winter.

Polar aircraft have skis to land on ice and snow.

Smallest ocean

The Arctic Ocean is the world's smallest and shallowest ocean. Its average depth is only 1000 metres. It is almost entirely surrounded by land, mainly the northern parts of North America, Europe and Asia. A few seas join the Arctic Ocean, including the Laptev Sea, Kara Sea, Barents Sea and Beaufort Sea.

Not all Arctic ice is solid. In summer, some of the ice cracks into thin, floating plates called floes.

Ice sheets

In winter, more than half of the Arctic Ocean is covered by a vast, floating sheet of ice, 2 to 3 metres thick. In summer, some of the ice cracks and melts, forming jumbled blocks of ice. These lumps make travel across the Arctic's ice sheets very difficult.

Wow!

At 14 million square kilometres, the Arctic Ocean is 13 times smaller than the largest ocean, the Pacific Ocean.

It's so... far!

Many explorers have tried to march across the floating ice to the North Pole, but failed. American Robert Peary and his team said they reached the North Pole in 1909, but some experts do not agree with this.

Winter ice extent

North America   Asia

North Pole

Greenland

Summer ice extent

North America   Asia

North Pole

Greenland

The Arctic ice sheet is twice as large in winter compared to summer.

The grey wolf has a thick coat to keep it warm.

Northern forests

About 2500 kilometres from the North Pole are the northern lands of North America, Europe and Asia. The vast forests in these regions are some of the largest in the world.

Tough conifers

The forests of the far north are called boreal forests, or taiga. The trees here are mainly **conifers**, including pines, firs, spruces and larches. These produce their seeds in woody **cones**. Most are **evergreen**, with leaves all year round. To survive frost and snow during the long, cold winter, the leaves of these hardy trees are formed into thin needles or hard scales.

The caribou, also called the reindeer, is only found in northern regions.

The rippling
Northern Lights
are seen in
skies around the
North Pole.

Wow!

The brown bear,
or grizzly, is the
world's largest land
meat eater. It can
weigh 800 to 1000
kilograms.

Northern forests are
covered in snow during
the winter months.

Forest animals

Plant-eating animals of the northern
forests include the snowshoe hare, the
caribou and the elk, as well as birds,
such as the grouse and the crossbill.
These are hunted by wolves, lynxes
and brown bears.

**It's so
beautiful!**

At night, the northern
skies are sometimes lit
by coloured, wavy glows
called the Northern Lights,
or *Aurora Borealis*.

Musk oxen grow a thick, warm fleece in winter.

In winter, the ptarmigan's white feathers help it to hide in the snow.

Treeless tundra

Between the northern forests and the shores of the Arctic Ocean to the north are tundra lands. There are no trees and they are covered in snow in winter.

Small plants and shrubs

The tundra is far too cold for trees to survive. Only small plants grow here, including mosses, lichens, tough grasses and herbs. Low-growing shrubs, such as arctic willow and birch, are also found. During the short summer, these plants provide food for animals, such as lemmings, musk oxen and ptarmigans.

Wow!

The musk ox has the longest fur of any animal. Some hairs are more than one metre in length!

The Sami people of northern Finland follow the caribou when it migrates.

Forest and tundra

In summer, caribou travel, or **migrate**, north onto the tundra to feed on the limited plant growth. In autumn, they migrate back south to the shelter of the forests. Other creatures, such as musk oxen and the Arctic fox, can stay on the tundra all year around.

Arctic poppies bloom in the short summer.

Icy shores

The shores of the Arctic Ocean are partly frozen during the long winter, although the ice melts in summer. These shores are home to many animals, including the polar bear.

Seals and walruses

Few plants grow along the shores of the Arctic Ocean. In the water, however, there is plenty of food, including fish and shellfish. These are eaten by large hunters, such as seals and long-tusked walruses.

It's so white!

The largest polar bear stood more than 3 metres tall and weighed more than ten adult people!

Wow!

Many Arctic animals, such as polar bears, snowy owls and Arctic foxes, are white so that they blend in with the ice and snow. This is called **camouflage**.

Walruses spend most of the year in the Arctic.

Polar bears

The largest predator along the Arctic shores is the polar bear. Although it mainly eats seals, the polar bear also feeds on seabirds, fish and even small whales. When it cannot find animals to eat, the polar bear will eat berries, mosses and other plants.

A mother polar bear teaches her young how to hunt.

The Arctic fox has the warmest fur of any mammal.

Each year, guillemots fly to the Arctic to breed.

13

Seas of the north

The Arctic Ocean is extremely cold, but contains plenty to eat. The small sea animals that live here are food for larger creatures, such as great whales and killer whales.

A mother harp seal returns from hunting to feed her pup.

Tiny floating plants

The Arctic Ocean is home to many kinds of seal and whale. Beluga and killer whales live here alongside larger whales, such as the northern right whale and the bowhead whale. These large sea **predators** feed on smaller creatures, which eat even smaller ones. These then feed on tiny plants called phytoplankton, which grow during the long hours of summer daylight.

Wow!

The bowhead whale has the largest mouth of any animal. Its mouth is up to 4 metres long – a quarter of its body length.

Thick blubber

Many sea animals need protection against the bitter cold of the Arctic Ocean. Whales, seals and walruses have a thick layer of fat under the skin, called blubber, to keep in body warmth.

Male narwhals display their tusk at breeding time.

The beluga, or white whale, grows up to 5 metres in length.

It's so sharp!

The narwhal whale stays in Arctic waters all year. The male's upper tooth grows into a long, sharp tusk that is used for fighting during the breeding season.

Visitors to the north

In summer, plants grow quickly in the Arctic. They provide food for animals that arrive each year for a few months.

Arctic terns snatch fish from just below the surface of the water.

Snow geese remember their migration route year after year.

Arctic migrants

Animals that make long journeys each year are called migrants. Many Arctic migrants are birds, such as terns, geese and ducks. They fly north in spring to nest on the tundra, feed on plants and small creatures, and raise their chicks. When the days get shorter in the cold autumn, they fly back south to warmer lands.

Wow!

Wow!

The Arctic tern spends one summer in the Arctic, before flying south for another summer in the Antarctic — a yearly journey of 35,000 kilometres.

Warmer waters

Sea animals that migrate to the Arctic for summer include blue whales, sperm whales and sea lions. Grey whales swim up the Pacific coast of North America in spring to feed near Alaska and in the Bering Sea. In autumn, they return south to have their babies in warmer waters.

The grey whale has small creatures called barnacles living on its head.

It's so long distance!

Grey whales make the longest migration of any mammal — a yearly trip of up to 20,000 kilometres.

The Antarctic: frozen land

Antarctica is at the opposite end of the world to the Arctic. It is a frozen land surrounded by ocean – the Arctic is a frozen ocean surrounded by land.

Wow!

Antarctica is more than 1.5 times the size of the USA.

Hidden mountains

Antarctica is a vast **landmass**, making up one-tenth of the world's land area. It is nearly all covered by a giant ice cap, which is an average of 2000 metres thick, although in some places it is up to 4500 metres thick. Under the ice are mountains, valleys and lakes.

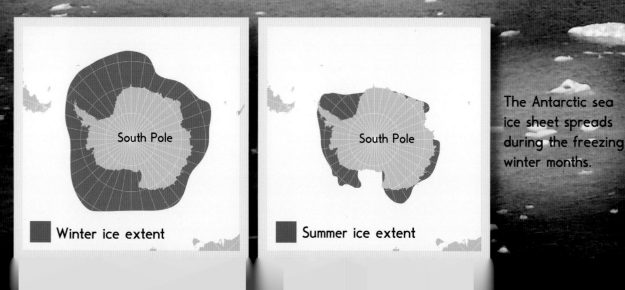

South Pole

South Pole

■ Winter ice extent

■ Summer ice extent

The Antarctic sea ice sheet spreads during the freezing winter months.

Cold, windy and dry

Antarctica is not only the coldest place on Earth, it is also the windiest. Its gale-force storms can last for weeks. It is also a desert. At the South Pole, near the middle of Antarctica, the snowfall is equal to just 2.5 centimetres of rain each year. This is not much more than the rainfall in parts of the Sahara Desert.

On 14 December 1911, Norwegian Roald Amundsen and his team were the first to reach the South Pole.

Antarctica's coast has steep cliffs and icy seas.

It's so... hidden!

Lake Vostok in the Antarctic is buried under 4 kilometres of ice and has not been visible for 40 million years.

King penguins rest on ice before diving into the cold water to hunt for fish.

Southern Ocean

Around Antarctica is the great Southern Ocean. It is 1.5 times bigger and much deeper than the Arctic Ocean. It teems with life in the summer months.

The Antarctic fin whale is 22 metres long and weighs up to 70 tonnes.

Wow!

Each day, a blue whale can eat more than four million shrimplike krill!

Food chain

The Southern Ocean, like the Arctic Ocean, is cold but rich in nutrients. During the summer months, when there is plenty of light, tiny phytoplankton grow. These are eaten by tiny zooplankton, which are in turn food for bigger creatures, such as fish and squid.

Antarctic fish have natural chemical 'antifreeze' in their blood.

Antarctic krill that are not eaten can live for up to six years.

Giant shoals of krill

One of the most important creatures in the Southern Ocean is the tiny krill, a cousin of the shrimp. Millions of krill come together to form giant shoals. They are eaten by all kinds of Antarctic animals, including seals, penguins and seabirds. Great whales, such as the blue and humpback whale, also feast on krill.

It's so common!

The crabeater seal is one of the world's most common seals, numbering about 30 million. But it does not eat crabs! It feeds mainly on krill and on small fish and squid.

The leopard seal has sharp front teeth for feeding on prey.

Islands of ice

Icebergs are massive lumps of ice that have broken off ice caps around polar lands. Antarctica has the biggest icebergs. Some are the size of small countries.

WOW!

The enormous male southern elephant seal can weigh up to 4000 kilograms – as heavy as an elephant!

Layers of ice

Over hundreds of years, the snow that has fallen on polar lands, such as Antarctica in the south and Greenland in the north, has been squashed into layers of ice. Gradually, these layers have been squeezed, causing them to slide off sideways towards the coast. At the coast, big lumps of ice break off into the ocean and drift away as icebergs.

Resting and hiding

Icebergs are like floating islands, and some can last for many years before melting away. They are ideal resting places for seabirds, such as petrels and penguins, as well as seals. Icebergs also contain handy hiding places. The leopard seal lurks around the edges of icebergs, waiting to grab a penguin or small seal that passes by.

Chinstrap penguins sometimes breed on icebergs.

Only one-eighth of an iceberg is above water.

The coldest place

Nowhere on Earth is as cold as Antarctica. Around its icy coasts, the average temperature is 0°C, and that is in summer!

Winter freeze

The ice melts in summer at a few places around the edge of Antarctica. Small plants can then grow, including mosses and lichens, and little flowers, such as the Antarctic pearlwort. The tiny creatures that live in the thin soil, such as the insect-like springtail, must survive being frozen all winter.

Wow!

Male emperor penguins can survive temperatures of minus 40°C, winds of more than 200 kilometres an hour and weeks of almost constant darkness.

It's so... far!

Some emperor penguins march more than 100 kilometres from the sea to their breeding site.

Emperor penguins

Amazingly, emperor penguins can live in Antarctica through the long, bitter winters. These penguins walk from the sea to their traditional breeding sites. The female lays an egg and goes back to sea to feed. The male keeps the egg warm on his feet and huddles with other males through the freezing winter. The females return two months later to help feed their new chicks.

Snow petrels breed further south than any other bird.

Emperor penguins huddle together to protect the chicks and keep them warm.

Young king penguins chicks are kept warm by their parents.

Polar people

People have lived in the Arctic region for thousands of years. Their traditional way of life makes every use of natural resources.

Inuit people hunt and fish in boats called kayaks.

Arctic dwellers

Many groups of people, such as the Yu'pik, Chukchi, Koryak, Aleuts and Inuit, live on the lands around the Arctic. They have developed skills to find food, make shelters and survive the cold. Much of their food comes from the sea in the form of fish, seals and whales. Caribou and other animals are also part of their diet.

It's so green!

When Viking explorers arrived in Greenland 1000 years ago, the climate was warmer and there were trees, shrubs and grass. They called the region 'Greenland'. Today, it is covered in ice.

A small harpoon head carved from ivory.

Wow!

People of the far north have many words for snow. For example, *mauja* is soft, deep snow, and *pukak* is powdery, loose snow.

An igloo is a temporary shelter made from snow blocks.

Skins and bones

Arctic creatures provide much more than food. The skins of seals and caribou are used to make clothes, boots and tents. Horns, tusks and baleen, or whalebone, are carved into kitchen utensils and tools. These are also used to craft jewellery and other items.

Protect the poles

Even though polar regions are far away, they are at risk from the effects of the modern world.

Mining for minerals

About 300 years ago, people began sailing to polar seas to kill seals, whales and other animals. They also explored the land for valuable **minerals**, such as oil, coal and precious gems. Today, oil wells and mines dot the land and oil spills from huge tanker ships have ruined some areas.

Cruise ships bring tourists to see polar wildlife.

It's so safe?

The Southern Ocean is a vast **sanctuary** where whales are protected. However, ships still catch fish, squid and krill, which means whales have less to eat.

Melting ice

Polar lands
and seas need
protection from
pollution. Dangerous
chemicals are spreading
in polar waters and the protective
ozone gas high in the sky has been
damaged by chemicals from aerosol spray
cans and fridges. Many scientists believe
that **global warming** is melting the polar
ice caps, destroying the natural **habitats**
of people and animals.

Wow!

If all the ice in the
polar ice caps melted,
sea levels would rise by
more than 50 metres. This
would flood many great
cities along shores
and coasts.

There are many oil pipelines and tankers in Alaska, USA.

Damage caused by oil
spills can last many years.

Glossary

Camouflage Colours and patterns that blend with the surroundings, making a creature difficult to see.

Conifers Trees that produce their seeds in cones.

Cones Hard, woody parts made by trees, such as pines and firs, which contain seeds.

Evergreen Trees that have some leaves all through the year.

Global warming Heating up of the Earth caused by changes in the gases that make up its atmosphere.

Habitats Types of places where animals and plants live, such as a wood, lake or seashore.

Landmass A large, continuous area of land.

Migrate To make a long journey each year to a place far away, and then to return again.

Minerals A large range of natural substances that make up rocks and soil.

Ozone gas A form of oxygen, which is high in the sky and helps protect against some of the sun's harmful rays.

Permafrost Soil that stays frozen all the time, not even thawing in summer.

Phytoplankton Tiny plants, mostly too small to see, that float in seas, oceans and large lakes.

Predator An animal that hunts others for food.

Sanctuary A safe, protected place.

Shoal A large gathering of water animals, such as fish or krill.

Zooplankton Tiny animals, mostly too small to see, that float in seas, oceans and large lakes.

Index